JAVA

Easy Java Programming for Beginners, Your Step-By-Step Guide to Learning Java Programming

Felix Alvaro

Acknowledgments

Firstly, I want to thank God for giving me the knowledge and inspiration to put this informative book together. I also want to thank my parents, my brothers and my partner Silvia for their support.

Table of Contents

Introduction

Hi there! Thank you for downloading this eBook. By doing so, you have made a big step in investing in your skills as a computer programmer! This eBook presents useful information on Java language suited for beginners. I am Felix and I also started as an amateur software programmer who has experienced the challenges in understanding basic Java terminologies and programming conventions. This eBook will then serve as an introduction to understanding the Java language and gear you towards your goal of becoming a professional computer programmer. I will be teaching you how to install the required Java tools and create simple programs in a step-by-step way.

At first glance, Java may come across as a language that will be hard to comprehend. After we get started, you will begin to familiarize yourself with the Java language environment and will quickly discover that it can be quite simple to learn after all! Regardless of your experience with programming languages, this guide will lead you in a way that is easy to follow and learn. As you expand your knowledge, the more you will appreciate the perks of being a Java programmer.

Java has always been considered as one of the top, in-demand programming languages in the world. If you decide to focus on studying the Java environment, then you are looking at a fast growing career. Such technology has been integrated and adopted widely in flourishing the World Wide Web, developing mobile apps, building websites and more. With its simplicity, readability and flexibility, Java has been one of the sought after programming skills in the recruitment market of Information Technology. Currently, a Java developer/programmer in the United States of America earns an estimated annual salary of $85,000 USD.

This eBook will definitely serve as your jumpstart if you decide to push a career in Java programming. I will provide you a discussion on the characteristics of the said software environment, the different components, terminologies, basic programming styles and sample programs, among others. You will find that Java programming is quite amusing, since it uses the normal English language in coding. So, let us get started!

Chapter One: History of Java

This chapter will give you a brief history of how Java software came into life, starting from the existence of computers. It will also provide you a brief overview of the evolution of the various computer programming languages.

The Birth of Computers

It was not long ago, well maybe around two decades, that there were still typewriters to create the documents we need at home, in school or for work. Remember your mother's recipes on index cards, your thesis in college, your resume for a job application and many more. Then here comes the birth of computer systems that made everything a whole lot easier! It was a total revolution when these miracle machines were introduced. Now, with just a click of the mouse or a keystroke you have photos printed out to decorate your home, a YouTube video of your high school ball, or a visually compelling marketing presentation for work.

A computer system consists of all the essential components of a computer and how they are integrated with one another for the device to function efficiently and effectively.

Such components can be classified as hardware or software. Computer hardware pertains to the physical part, such as the central processing unit (CPU), mouse, keyboard and monitor, among others. Software, on the other hand, refers to the different programs that tell the computer what to do. Both hardware and software components work hand in hand to produce the user's desired results.

Since this eBook was written to provide a step-by-step tutorial on Java programming, then we will emphasize on the software aspect of the computer system. In addition, the emergence of the World Wide Web or simply known as the Internet had brought forth more innovations in computer programming. The increasing demands of this online superhighway when it comes to sharing and communicating information has forced programmers to explore the potentials of JAVA programming language.

Evolution of Computer Programming Languages

- 1954-1957

  John Backus with an IBM team developed FORTRAN (considered the first modern computer programming language but definitely not user-friendly).

- 1959

  Grace Hopper at Remington Rand developed COBOL (Letter B stands for Business, which is COBOL's primary feature that included processing records of customers, employees and more)

- 1972

  Dennis Ritchie at AT&T Bell Labs developed the C programming language.

- 1986

  Bjarne Stroustrup at AT&T Bell Labs developed C++ that supported object-oriented programming (OOP).

- 1995

  It was exactly on May 23rd that Sun Microsystems released the first official version of Java programming language that is considered as an improvement of C++. This general-purpose software enables you to build and explore databases, write windowed applications and control handheld devices, among others. Just after five years, Java already had 2.5 million developers worldwide.

- 2000

  The College Board announced in November that Computer Science Advanced Placement exams will be based on Java by 2003.

- 2002

  Microsoft introduced C#, a new language named that inherited most of its programming features from Java. Sys-Con Media reported in June of the same year that there was an increasing demand for Java programmers (it has exceeded by 50% as compared to the demand for C++ programmers).

- 2007

  Google started developing apps on Android mobile devices using the Java language.

- 2010

  Oracle Corporation incorporated Java technology into the Oracle family by purchasing Sun Microsystems in January

- 2010

  eWeek ranked Java in June as first among its "Top 10 Programming Languages to Keep You Employed" (www.eweek.com/c/a/ Application-Development/Top-10-

Programming-Languagesto-Keep-You-Employed-719257).

- 2013

  More than 1.1 billion desktop computers and 250 million mobile phones have been using Java platform since August 2013 (www.mobiledevicemanager.com/mobile-devicestatistics/250-million-android-devices-in-use and http://java.com/en/about). Moreover, Blu-ray devices emerged with more interactive capabilities through the new technology. Java was already considered the most popular language by various programming groups and communities, such as TIOBE Programming Community Index (www.tiobe.com/index.php/ content/paperinfo/tpci) and PYPL that stands for the PopularitY of Programming Language Index (http://sites.google.com/site/pydatalog/ pypl/PyPL-PopularitY-of-Programming-Language), among others.

Emergence of Java Technology

When IT experts realized in the early 1990s that there is a big demand in making people's lives less complicated by introducing intelligence to everyday home appliances, Sun Microsystems collaborated with a team of researchers to start the "Green Project". This is sort of a secretive assignment aimed to develop a portable home-appliance software that will run in embedded processor chips. The program should be flexible enough to adapt to the ever-changing appliance processor chips, which were getting smaller, cheaper and yet more powerful. The team planned to use C++ at first, but its portability issue was blocking their path to success. Thus, they decided to develop a whole new computer programming language.

It was in 1991 when Java language was initially conceived by Sun Microsystem through the collaboration of James Gosling, Chris Warth, Patrick Naughton, Mike Sheridan and Ed Frank. Oak was the initial name of the new programming language, which was the tree just outside James Gosling's window (the team's project leader). However, Oak was already being used as the name for another programming language. So in 1995 it was officially renamed to Java, which denotes the coffee that the software developers enjoy whenever they have their breaks. However, when the demand for such home-appliances did not turn out as what Sun Microsystem expected, the programming team has to find another channel to expand Java. Finally, in May 1995, Java was first released at the SunWorld Conference and was immediately followed by Netscape (the world's #1 browser at that time) announcing that they will incorporate the programming language in their development. With Java-embedded web pages, websites transformed from plain dull into interactive ones. Not only that the Web sends information to its audience, but they are also able to accept user input.

In this chapter you have learned the history of computer programming languages, focusing on the development of Java technology. In the succeeding chapter, Java will be described on how it is used in various programming environments with a clear instruction on how to properly install it in your computer.

Chapter Two: The Java Environment

Getting a closer look on Java programming, this chapter will start its discussion on how you can use and deploy the software in various environments. It will also present a step-by-step instruction on how to install, not only the Java program itself but also other required tools on your computer.

With the unstoppable growth of the World Wide Web, developers have found ways on how to incorporate Java programs on every web page. The following is a summary on how the software language is used in different environments:

- **Applet** - A type of networked Java program embedded in a Web page that is automatically executed by another Java-compatible browser when transmitted over the Internet. Usually this is a small program that can display data from the server, manage user input or even perform simple functions like a calculator. These functionalities are done locally on the client's computer instead of connecting to the server, which means when you click an applet link it will be automatically downloaded and run in the browser.

- **Servlet** - A type of small Java program that supports a browser but runs on a different computer or web server to extend its functionality. The introduction of the servlet has upgraded the client/server connection.

- **JavaServer Page (JSP)** - A Web page that consists of fragments of a Java program (as opposed to an applet that has the complete program).

- **Micro Edition (ME) Java Application** - A Java program running on a resource device with a limited amount of memory, such as a mobile phone or a television set-top box.

- **Standard Edition (SE) Java Application** - A Java program that runs on a standard computer, such as a desktop or a laptop.

- **JavaFX** - A Java program that is integrated with multimedia platforms, such as Flash players.

The Initial Java Setup

Before you sit in front your computer and start coding, you need to make sure that you and your machine are equipped for writing Java codes. It is strongly advised that you check out the following websites and follow the instructions in downloading the required software that is usually for free:

For Java software download and installation follow the following steps:

1. Go to the website http://java.com by typing this in the address bar of your web browser. It will take you to the screen below:

2. Click on the **FREE JAVA DOWNLOAD** button. It will take you to this screen:

3. Click on the **AGREE AND START FREE DOWNLOAD** button. When your Java download is complete, you have to close all your browsers and reload them to enable the Java installation.

4. Run the downloaded file and you will get the screen below. Just click the **INSTALL** button.

- www.oracle.com/technetwork/java/javase/downloads - Download and install the required Java SE documentation (also known as the Javadoc pages or Java SE API Docs)

Next:

1. Go to the website
   www.oracle.com/technetwork/java/javase/downloads ,
   It will take you to the screen below:

2. Click on this option

Java Platform (JDK) 8u65 / 8u66

3. The next page will ask you to choose the version of
   Java SE Development Kit you want to download.
   Make sure you know exactly what operating system
   you have in your computer or laptop before you start
   downloading.

4. To check the version of your operating system, you can go to the **SYSTEMS** or **PC INFO** settings of your computer/laptop.

5. Open the downloaded program to complete the installation of your Jave SE Development Kit. Ensure that you read and follow the steps carefully.

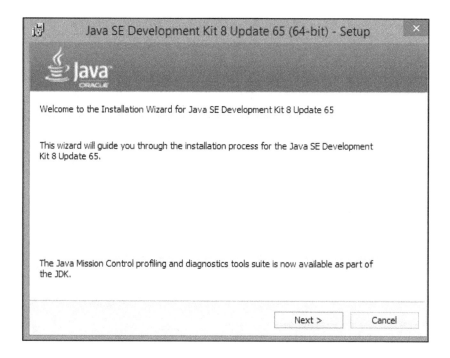

- http://eclipse.org/downloads - Download and install the Eclipse program you need

Then;

1. Go to the website http://eclipse.org/downloads by typing this in the address bar of your web browser. It will take you to the screen below:

2. Choose the appropriate version of Eclipse based on your computer's operating system. For a 64-bit Windows operating system (OS), you will get the screen below:

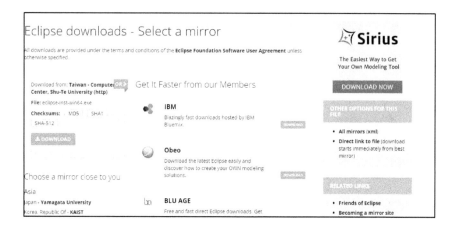

3. After downloading, open the program and you will get the screen below:

4. Just choose **ECLIPSE IDE FOR JAVA DEVELOPERS** option and then click the **INSTALL** button. Make sure you accept the **ECLIPSE FOUNDATION SOFTWARE USER AGREEMENT**.

After downloading the programs, make sure you test your installed software. You can follow these steps to test Eclipse:

- Launch Eclipse. You should be able to see an **ECLIPSE JAVA MARS** icon on the desktop. It will then ask you to **SELECT A WORKSPACE**. Just leave what is inside the box and then click the **OK** button.

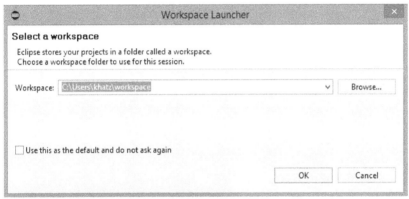

- Create a new Java project by going to the menu on top:
  FILE > NEW > JAVA PROJECT

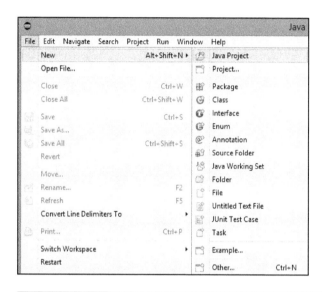

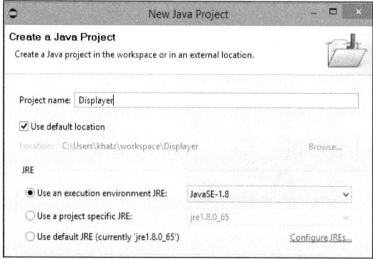

- Create a new class named **Displayer** within the Java project.

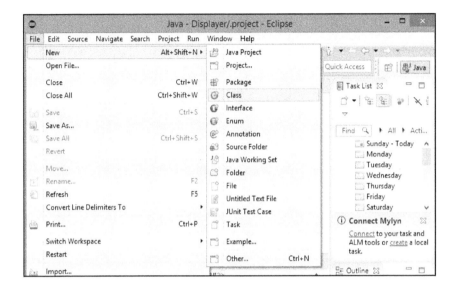

- Modify the new **Displayer.java** file by entering the following lines of code in the Editor pane.

public class Displayer {

    public static void main(String args[]) {

        System.out.println("Hello Java!");

    }

}

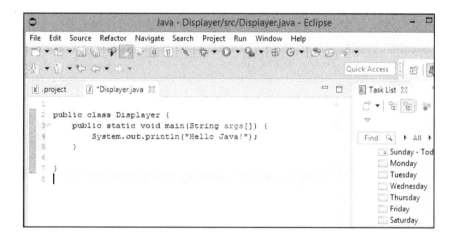

- Execute **Displayer.java** by clicking on this button located at the top and check to make sure that the output reads **Hello Java!** by checking the figure below.

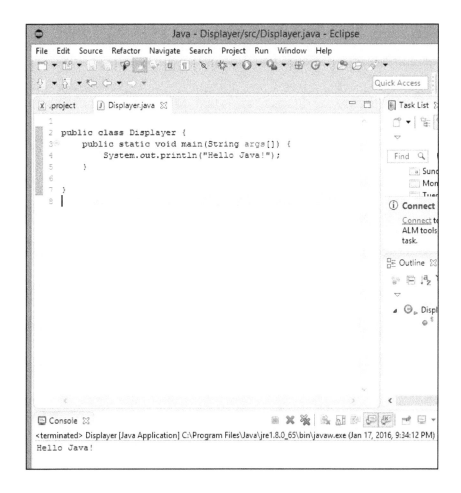

In the field of computer programming, software developers require existing programs to create new programs. For example, you want to develop a Java program that will handle your company's employee records. In order to accomplish this, you might use an existing program as an error-checking tool for your Java codes.

Required Java Tools

Below are the different tools needed in Java programming that can be downloaded online for free:

- **Compiler**

    A compiler turns the Java code you write into something that can be understood and run on your computer. Computers do not comprehend instructions same like humans. For example, check the program code below:

Looking for an available rental car:

```java
// This is part of a Java program
// (not a complete Java program).
rentalcarNum = 1;
while (rentalcarNum < 100) {
   if (client[rentalcarNum] == 0) {
            out.println("Car " + rentalcarNum
                  + " is available.");
   exit(0);
   } else {
            rentalcarNum ++;
   }
}
out.println("All cars or vehicles are rented out");
```

This basic Java code searches for any available rental car or vehicle for a certain client, assuming that the company has 99 cars in total. You cannot run this code by just typing as it is. However, ignoring the strange punctuations and typing format, human beings are able to grasp what it wants the computer to do:

Set the rental car number to 1.
As long as the rental car number is less than 100,
        Check the number of clients that rented the
car.
                If the number of clients that rented
        the car is 0, then
                report that the car is available,
                and stop.
        Otherwise,
                prepare to check the next car by
                adding 1 to rental car number.
        If you get to the non-existent rental car number
100, then
                report that all cars or vehicles were rented
        out.

As for computers, they do not follow English-translated instructions to do a specific task. Instead, they understand cryptic Java bytecode commands. This is where the compiler comes in. After writing your Java source code, it is being translated and written by the compiler into Java bytecodes that the computer can execute.

Check bytecode counterpart below for the same Java code:

```
aload_0
iconst_1
putfield Company/ rentalcarNum I
goto 32
aload_0
getfield Company/client [I
aload_0
getfield Company/rentalcarNum I
iaload
ifne 26
getstatic java/lang/System/out
Ljava/io/PrintStream;
new java/lang/StringBuilder
dup
ldc " Car "
invokespecial
java/lang/StringBuilder/<init>(Ljava/lang/String;)V
aload_0
getfield Company/rentalcarNum I
invokevirtual
java/lang/StringBuilder/append(I)Ljava/lang/StringBuilde
r;
ldc " is available."
invokevirtual
        java/lang/StringBuilder/append(Ljava/lang/
String;)Ljava/lang/StringBuilder;
invokevirtual
java/lang/StringBuilder/toString()Ljava/lang/String;
```

```
            invokevirtual
java/io/PrintStream/println(Ljava/lang/String;)V
            iconst_0
            invokestatic java/lang/System/exit(I)V
            goto 32
            aload_0
            dup
            getfield Company/rentalcarNum I
            iconst_1
            iadd
            putfield Company/rentalcarNum I
            aload_0
            getfield Company/rentalcarNum I
            bipush 100
            if_icmplt 5
            getstatic java/lang/System/out
Ljava/io/PrintStream;
            ldc " All cars or vehicles are rented out"
            invokevirtual
java/io/PrintStream/println(Ljava/lang/String;)V
            return
```

The source code can be saved in a file named Company.java and the compiler probably puts the Java bytecode in another file named Company.class. You even need a tool to display a text-like version of a Java bytecode file (you can use Ando Saabas's Java Bytecode Editor). If you try open the code of the Company.class file using Notepad or even Microsoft Word, you will only see gibberish characters like dots, squiggles and more.

Java Virtual Machine (JVM)

If the compiler is responsible for writing the Java bytecode, then the Java Virtual Machine is in-charge of deciphering it. In reality, each kind of computer processor has its own set of executable instructions that are interpreted by each operating system in a slightly different way. Let's take a look at the two programs below for two different processors but will display the same output on the computer screen – "Hello world!".

Simple Program- Pentium Processor

```
.data
msg:
  .ascii "Hello, world!\n"
  len = . - msg
.text
  .global _start
_start:
  movl $len,%edx
  movl $msg,%ecx
  movl $1,%ebx
  movl $4,%eax
  int $0x80
  movl $0,%ebx
  movl $1,%eax
  int $0x80
```

Simple Program- Powerpc Processor

```
.data
msg:
        .string "Hello, world!\n"
        len = . - msg
.text
        .global _start
_start:
        li      0,4

        li      3,1


        lis     4,msg@ha

        addi    4,4,msg@l

        li      5,len

        sc


        li      0,1

        li      3,1

        sc
```

These two programs ought to display the same results but they cannot be interchanged, for the instructions will mean nothing when they are run by the wrong processor. You will either get notification or error messages like "Not a valid Win32 application" or "Windows can't open this file." That is why, with the help of Java Virtual Machine, these Java bytecodes create order in this chaotic world of programming! JVM acts like an interpreter that translates those bytecodes for any computer system to comprehend. Thus, you do not have to worry because whether it is your computer or your friend's one, both will be able to run the bytecode. Thus, Java language has solved the issue of portability and versatility through JVM.

Integrated Development Environment

The early days of Java programming involved opening several windows – one for typing the code, another for running the program, and maybe a third one to keep track of all the codes you have written. What a messy situation! With the emergence of the integrated development environment (IDE) all of the functionalities were seamlessly combined into a single well-organized application.

Below are some of the most popular Java IDEs that can be downloaded online for free (their features may vary but still the language remains exactly the same):

1. Eclipse (www.eclipse.org)

Regarded as one of the most popular and best-looking interfaces because of its interactive design and navigation features, Eclipse is characterized as a user-friendly and open source software.

2. NetBeans (https://netbeans.org)

Just like the previous program, this open source IDE is one of the most recommended Java programming environments for beginners. It is also fast and powerful that can support all Java platforms from Standard Edition (SE) to FX.

3. BlueJ (http://bluej.org/)

BlueJ is described to have the simplest IDE interface and specifically designed to help a novice user understand the fundamental concepts of Java programming.

4. DrJava (www.drjava.org)

DrJava was also designed for amateur programmers who want a simple interface. Despite its simplicity, it is still powerful enough for proficient Java programmers.

5. Jave Development Kit (JDK)

The Java Development Kit is a tool that acts as both a compiler and an interpreter. The latest JDK version can be downloaded from Oracle's website - www.oracle.com/technetwork/java/javase/downloads/index.html. Ensure that you download the appropriate version for your computer. If you are using a 32-bit operating system, then download the matching file name affixed with x86. Otherwise, if it is a 64-bit operating system then download the one with x64.

Now, we have learned that Java can be deployed in a multitude of ways. This chapter also gave you a clear set of instructions on how to install the software and all other required tools for the program to run properly. In the next chapter, you will experience how to start coding in a Java environment.

Chapter Three: The Basics of Java Code

Before you start writing lines of Java code, this chapter will describe first what object-oriented programming is all about (which is one of the primary characteristics of Java programming). You will also encode your first simple Java program and understand the importance of every part. Also, you will be introduced to classes, objects and instances.

One must understand that the heart of Java language methodology is object-oriented programming (OOP). Over the years, software developers are progressively trying to find ways on how decrease the complexity of encoding programs. The first generation of programming languages involved toggling of binary machine codes, which are only a few hundred instructions long, into the computer's front panel. When programs evolved that required IT experts to handle more complex instructions through symbolic representations, then the assembly language was developed. As programming methodologies were enhanced, more high-level languages were introduced. One example is FORTRAN, however, codes were not easy-to-understand yet.

Structured programming emerged during the 1960s that was used in C and Pascal languages. These programs were characterized by local variables, rich control constructs and stand-alone subroutines, among others. Even if they were considered as power tools, they are still limited when handling very large projects.

The demand for breaking through the barriers of encoding extremely large projects paved way to the advent of object-oriented programming. It is a combination of the best methodologies of structured programming plus new organizing concepts. This programming style is characterized by the following:

- Encapsulation

    By the name itself, encapsulation is a strategy that binds the programming code and the data it manipulates and keeps them safe from outside interference. When code and data are linked together, an object is created. This object contains code and data that are either private or public. A private code or data cannot be accessed by any program that exists outside the said object. When it is public, then the other parts of the program are able to access even if they are not within the object.

- Polymorphism

  This concept is often described as creating a single interface for multiple methods. It means you design a generic interface to a group of related activities. It further reduces the complexity of the program by letting the same interface to be used to specify a general class of action. A clear analogy is the steering wheel. No matter what type of steering wheel, whether a manual steering or a power steering, as long as you know how it works then you can drive any type of car.

- Inheritance

  This process involves one object acquiring the properties of another object, which supports the concept of hierarchical classification. To better explain this, imagine a red delicious watermelon which belongs to the classification watermelon. The watermelon is further part of the fruit class, which belongs to a larger class called food. The food class has certain qualities such as edible and nutritious, that is further applied to its subclass fruit. The fruit has certain qualities as well, such as juicy and sweet. Now for the watermelon, it also has attributes specific to it, such as a tropical vine-like plant. Now combining all these qualities makes a unique red delicious watermelon.

Object-oriented programming is characterized by the application and organization of **classes**, **objects** and **instances**. These are actually the components that make up a Java program and are interconnected with one another.

- Class - Considered as the highest group, class encompasses everything in object-oriented programming.

- Object - Specifications set by the classes are being applied to the objects that are not loaded into the computer's memory. They are also instances of a class that act as blueprints ready to be used when needed. Thus, one class can have any number of objects associated with it (can even have zero objects).

- Instance - Can be the same as objects since they describe an individual instantiation.

To understand their relationship with one another, imagine that you are developing a computer program that will keep track of the students enrolling in a school. Each student has a distinctive feature – hair style, eye color, skin complexion, height, weight and many more. In your OOP program, each student is an **object**. Now, even if the students differ from one another, they share the same list of physical features. These attributes or characteristics need to be compiled into a master list, which we call a **class**.

First Simple Java Program

Let us try again to encode a short sample program by following these instructions:

1. Launch Eclipse. Click **FILE > NEW > JAVA PROJECT**. Name your new project as **EXAMPLE**.

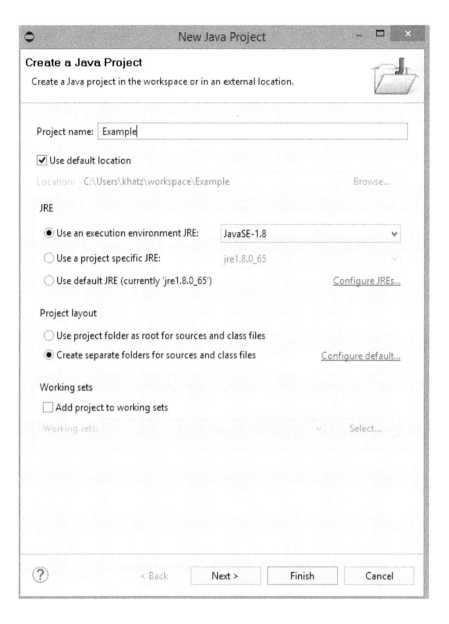

2. Create a new **EXAMPLE** class. Click **FILE > NEW > CLASS** > Type **EXAMPLE** for the class name.

3. Enter, compile and run the following program:

```
File   Edit   Source   Refactor   Navigate   Search   Project   Run   Window   Help

X .project      J Example.java

1  /*
2   * This is a simple Java program.
3   *
4   * Call this file Example.java
5   */
6  public class Example {
7  // A Java program begins with a call to main().
8      public static void main(String args[]){
9          System.out.println("Java is essential to the Web");
10     }
11 }
12 |

Console
<terminated> Example [Java Application] C:\Program Files\Java\jre1.8.0_65\bin\javaw.exe (Jan 17, 2016, 11:57:04 PM)
Java is essential to the Web
```

Encoding the Java program

In Java, a source file is called a compilation unit and the name that you give a source file is very important. By convention, the name of the main class should match the name of the file that holds the program. Take note that Java programming is case sensitive, which means the compiler distinguishes between lowercase and uppercase letters. Also, the filename extension required by the compiler is **.java**. Following this programming convention makes it easier to organize and keep track of your lines of code. Also, if you change the capitalization or the naming convention, then the whole program becomes meaningless and

48

will stop working. So for this activity, we named it **Example.java** (since the public class defined by the program is also **Example**).

Compiling the Java Program

In this stage, the compiler **javac** is being executed and creates a file called **Example.class** that contains the bytecode version of the program. In the previous discussion, the bytecode is executed by the Java Virtual Machine. To actually run the program, use the Java interpreter called **java** by passing the class name **Example** as a command-line argument as shown below:

java Example

The following output is displayed when the program is run:

Java is essential to the Web

During compilation, each individual class is placed into its own output file named after the class with **.class** extension. It has been a convention to name your Java source file the same name as the class file so that when you execute the Java interpreter, you are actually specifying the name of the class that you want to be executed.

Parts of the Java Program

- **Comments**

Comments are the descriptive parts of the program that explain what the codes are all about. They are special sections of text that improve the program's readability - helping people understand the operation of the program. Basically, these are the words that we humans read but the compiler totally ignores. There are two types of comments, depending on how you write them:

1. **One-Line or End-of-Line Comment**

Starting with two slashes, this comment text is short enough to fit on one line. It is also written at the end of a line of code. In the previous simple Java program example, the one-line comment that we have is:

// A Java program begins with a call to main ().

Everything is ignored by the compiler starting from the first slash up to the end of the line.

2. Block or Multi-Line Comment

This type is characterized by multiple one-line comments (meaning, your comment text is too long to fit in one line). However, the two slashes are replaced with an opening "/*" at the start of the comment and ends with a closing "*/" (to save time in writing "//" for every line). Again, the compiler ignores everything between the two slashes. In the previous simple Java program example, we have:

```
/*

* This is a simple Java program
*
* Call this file Example.java
*/
```

Prologue is a version of a block comment that is placed at the top or very beginning of your programs. It contains important information about the code so that every programmer will be able to get an idea what the program is all about just by merely glancing at it. Usually, the prologue is enclosed in a box of asterisks and includes the following information: filename, programmer's name and program description. If we are to modify the block comment above, it will look like this:

```
/*************************************************
*************************

* Example.java

* Felix & Khatz

*

* This is a simple program that displays "Java is
essential to the Web" on your PC screen

**************************************************
***************************/
```

- **Class Heading**

We now move to the next line in our first simple Java program:

```
public class Example {
```

This program line is called the **class heading** or **class declaration**, which is composed of 4 parts – the 3 words and the open curly brace (actually the entire program is considered as a class). Let's discuss each one of them.

The first two words, **public** and **class** are what we call *reserved words* or *keywords*. Such words are used for a particular purpose as defined by the Java language. You cannot redefine or use them to mean something else, like making them as names for your program. Below is a list of the common keywords in Java language:

abstract	assert	boolean	Break	Byte
case	catch	char	Class	const
continue	default	do	double	else
enum	extends	final	finally	float
for	goto	if	Implements	import
instanceof	int	interface	Long	native
new	package	private	Protected	public
return	short	static	strictfp	super
switch	synchronized	this	Throw	throws
transient	try	void	volatile	while

Analyzing each word, **class** is a marker that signifies the start of the class or the beginning of the program. It also states that a new class is being defined. In our first simple program, **Example** is the name of the class. On the other hand, **public** is an access modifier that controls how the class is being accessed (in this case, the information can be accessed by all other classes). If it was set to **private** instead of public, then only the current class has the access to it. Finally, the open curly brace "{" indicates the beginning of the class and has a corresponding closing brace "}" at the end of the entire program. Always coming in pairs, braces identify groupings of code for both the programmer and the computer.

- **Main Method's Heading**

After the class heading, the main method heading comes next. Method is a subroutine in Java language that is the line of code at which the program will begin executing. It is simply a list of things to do. In our example, the main method has the following form:

public static void main(String args[]) {

Again, **public** is an access modifier keyword, which indicates that everyone can access the main method. This also means that this can be accessed by the code outside the class in which it was defined or declared. **Static**, also another reserved word, denotes that the method can be accessed immediately. The third reserved word is **void** that signifies the main method returns nothing (in some programs it could return a value).

Any information that is needed to pass to a method is received by variables specified within the set of parentheses that follow the name of the method. These variables are also called parameters and in our example it is only **(String args[])**. The declared parameter named **args** represents the arguments that the main method takes. **String** is the argument's type that stores sequences of characters. The square brackets "[]" symbolizes that it is an array of objects of type strings. Even if there are no parameters required, you still need to indicate the empty parentheses.

- **System.out.println**

Based on our first simple Java program example, our main method contains the following line:

System.out.println("Java is essential to the Web");

System.out.println is a programming code that gives instructions to the computer to print something out. Let us discuss every part of it. **System** refers to the computer and when it becomes **System.out** it pertains to the monitor, which is the output device of the computer system. The next word, **println** (read as "print line") is a built-in Java method that is in control of printing computer messages. Overall, the line of code is what it refers to as **println method call**. You simply call a method when you want to execute it. Please remember that the first letter of a method call is always in uppercase and the rest will be in lowercase.

The text enclosed in double quotation marks inside the parentheses is the message to be printed out to the screen. These double quotes are in charge of grouping the messages together. At the end of the line is a semi-colon that signifies the end of the method call or programming statement (it is like period in the normal English language). All programming statements to be executed in Java end with a semicolon.

This chapter gave you a guide on how to start encoding using the Java programming language. You also have a better picture of what are the different parts of a simple program. In the next chapter, you will take programming to a higher level by incorporating what you call a user input.

Chapter Four: User Input

In this chapter the concept of user input will be introduced and incorporated into your Java programming language.

Based from the first simple Java program that we discussed earlier, you were not being asked to provide any form of input for the code execution. The lines of code just displayed the message on the computer screen. In the real world, programming requires a stable communication between the user and the machine. In Java language, this is what we call Input/Output or I/O streams. In this scenario a two-way communication is created where the user provides an input for the computer to process and then produces an output in return.

Getting the User Input

There is a built-in class called **Scanner** in Java language to easily get the user input. What it does is it acquires information from the input stream, either from the keyboard or a file, and stores in a variable. However, the Scanner class is not part of the core Java language so you need to tell the compiler where to find it. For you to use this, you need to include this line of code at the top of your program, just after the prologue section:

import java.util.Scanner;

Because of the additional statement, the Scanner class is being imported from the java.util package. To call or execute this class in the program, you need to use the following statement:

Scanner InputVariableName = new Scanner(System.in);

Now, the imported class Scanner was called to initialize a variable called **InputVariableName** (you can change this name to whatever you like but make sure it is not a Java keyword). This is followed by the assignment operator "=" that is in turn followed by the programming code **new Scanner(System.in);**. This expression creates an object and commands the program to store the value of the user input to **InputVariableName**. Please take note of the coding convention in variable naming: first letter of the words are always capitalized.

For us to utilize the output stream to show you what you have typed into the program, we need to include the following print out statement:

System.out.println(InputVariableName.nextLine());

The method **nextLine()** is included here that will instruct the program to return a string value that was inserted into the current line. It also tells the program to wait until it finishes searching for an input, so the program will not advance until you type something and press the Enter key on the keyboard. Let us further modify the println method by including an additive operator:

System.out.println("You entered " +
InputVariableName.nextLine());

At this point, the output statement contains a textual information that will be printed out together with the Scanner variable. The messages are combined using the additive operator "+" found inside the parentheses. Now, when the user provides an input, like for example "Johnny", then the program will display "You entered Johnny" on the computer screen.

Our modified program will actually look like this:

```
                                          Java - Example/src/Example.java - Eclipse
File  Edit  Source  Refactor  Navigate  Search  Project  Run  Window  Help

   project       Example.java

   /*
    * This is a simple Java program.
    *
    * Call this file Example.java
    */
   import java.util.Scanner;
   public class Example {
   // A Java program begins with a call to main().
       public static void main(String args[]){
           System.out.println("Java is essential to the Web");
           System.out.println("What is your name?");
           Scanner InputVariableName = new Scanner(System.in);
           System.out.println("You entered " + InputVariableName.nextLine());
       }
   }


   Console
<terminated> Example [Java Application] C:\Program Files\Java\jre1.8.0_65\bin\javaw.exe (Jan 22, 2016, 4:06:21 PM)
Java is essential to the Web
What is your name?
Johnny
You entered Johnny
```

From the program above, the message "What is your name?" is displayed to prompt you to enter your name. After you have typed your name and pressed enter (see the text in green located in the Console Section), the program will display your name after the words "You entered " on the screen.

The introduction of user input as described on this chapter had presented Java environment as a two-way form of communication – between the software programmer and the computer. You, as the user, will provide information for the computer to process through the execution of the lines of Java code. The succeeding chapter will now introduce the concept of variable declaration.

Chapter Five: Variable Declaration

Previously, we declared a variable to contain a text user input. If you want to create more complex programs then you have to store values in variables. This chapter will now focus on declaring variables as part of your programming style.

Assigning what type of variable to be used is done in a declaration statement with the following syntax:

<type> <list-of-variables-separated-by-commas>;

Examples:

int rows, cols;

String companyName;

Again, a variable is a placeholder, the thing stored in it is a value and the kind of value that is stored in a variable is its type. Looking at the declaration statements above, the word at the left (int, String) specifies the type for the variable or variables at the right (rows, cols, companyName). By the way, a Java variable can hold only one type of value and its value can change during program execution. So in the examples above, rows and cols variables can hold only integers while the second declaration statement the companyName variable can hold only strings. Below are the basic variable types in Java language:

Type Name	Description	Range of Values
Whole Number Types		
int (Integer)	- simplest data type for handling numbers - no decimal points - not ideal for precision data - default value is 0	-2147483648 to 2147483647
Byte	- has the smallest range for number data type - contains an 8-bit signed 2s complement integer - default value is 0	-128 to 127
Short	- contains 16-bit signed 2s integer - default value is 0	-32768 to 32767

long	- contains 64-bit signed 2s complement integer - default value is 0	-922337203685477 5808 to 922337203685477 5807
Decimal Number Types		
Float	- contains 32-bit IEEE 754 numerical values - contains decimal points - default value is 0.0f	-3.4×10^{38} to 3.4×10^{38}
Double	- contains 64-bit IEEE 754 numerical values - contains decimal points - more precise than float - default value is 0.0d	-1.8×10^{308} to 1.8×10^{308}
Character Type		

string	- contains a sequence of alphanumeric characters - default value is null	
Char	- accepts a single character as data - default value is \u0000 (represents an empty space)	thousands of characters and symbols
Logical Type		
boolean	- default value is False	True, False

Please take note of the following declaration statements for each variable type:

int AnyVariable;   or   int AnyVariable = 0;

byte AnyVariable;   or   byte AnyVariable = 0;

short AnyVariable;   or   short AnyVariable = 0;

long AnyVariable;   or   long AnyVariable = 0L;

float AnyVariable;   or   float AnyVariable = 0.0f;

double AnyVariable;   or   double AnyVariable = 0.0d;

String AnyVariable;   or   String AnyVariable = null;

char AnyVariable;

Boolean AnyVariable; or   Boolean AnyVariable = false;

As you can notice, String and Boolean are in uppercase letters. This is because they are data types that happen to be a class names too. Therefore, in code and conventional text we will use uppercase S and B.

Previously our Example Java program accepts a string value from the user. This time, we will alter the code so it will ask the user to enter an integer data type. Let us say the program will display the user's age after entering it. Take a look at the new programming code below:

```
                                                    Java - Example/src/Example.java
File  Edit  Source  Refactor  Navigate  Search  Project  Run  Window  Help

  project        Example.java
/*
 * This is a simple Java program.
 *
 * Call this file Example.java
 */
import java.util.Scanner;
public class Example {
// A Java program begins with a call to main().
    public static void main(String args[]){
        System.out.println("Java is essential to the Web");
        System.out.println("How old are you?");
        Scanner InputVariableName = new Scanner(System.in);
        System.out.println("Your age is " + InputVariableName.nextInt());
    }
}

Console
<terminated> Example [Java Application] C:\Program Files\Java\jre1.8.0_65\bin\javaw.exe (Jan 25, 2016, 9:10:50 PM)
Java is essential to the Web
How old are you?
35
Your age is 35
```

In the last programming line, we used nextInt() to instruct the program to save an integer data type. Other data types that we can also scan are nextByte(), nextShort(), nextLong(), nextFloat() and nextDouble().

If you need to create more complex operations in your programs that require using multiple input values, then it is better to save the user input and declare the variable. In this case, it is must that you already have an idea of what the data type of that variable should be. By modifying the program above, we will now have:

```
File  Edit  Source  Refactor  Navigate  Search  Project  Run  Window  Help
```

```
/*
 * This is a simple Java program.
 *
 * Call this file Example.java
 */
import java.util.Scanner;
public class Example {
// A Java program begins with a call to main().
    public static void main(String args[]){

        int MyVariableName = 0;
        System.out.println("Java is essential to the Web");
        System.out.println("How old are you?");
        Scanner InputVariableName = new Scanner(System.in);
        MyVariableName = InputVariableName.nextInt();
        System.out.println("Your age is " + MyVariableName);
    }
}
```

Console

<terminated> Example [Java Application] C:\Program Files\Java\jre1.8.0_65\bin\javaw.exe (Jan 25, 2016, 10:20:18 PM)
```
Java is essential to the Web
How old are you?
35
Your age is 35
```

Based on the new program code, the Scanner variable
InputVariableName was first saved into MyVariableName and
then was used to display the user-generated input to the screen.

After you have learned the different variable types and how
to properly declare them, you will now be able to create programs
with additional functionalities and complexities. In the following
chapter, another feature will be introduced which is the
application of the Java language operator.

Chapter Six: Operators

This chapter will describe the available operators that you can add to your lines of code as you program more complex scenarios. Operators are mainly used to control, modify and compare data in a Java language environment.

Since the beginning of this book, we have already been using the equal sign (=) or the assignment operator, which works by assigning a compatible value into a variable. In addition, arithmetic operators are used to control the value that will be assigned to a variable. If you can remember the mathematical operators you have learned in school, they will be the same operators you will need to perform mathematical computation in Java programming. Gaining the knowledge on how to use operators is an important requirement. All you need to understand are the symbols for each operator and their functions.

Arithmetic Operators

These are the most basic form of operators apart from the assignment operator.

Additive Operator (+)   – Returns the sum of two values

Subtractive Operator (-)   – Returns the difference of two values

Multiplicative Operator (*)   – Returns the product of two values

Divisive Operator (/)   – Returns the quotient of two values

Remainder Operator (%)   – Returns the remainder of two values being divided

Increment/Decrement Operators

These operators increase or decrease the value of the variable by 1.

Increment (++)   - Increase the value by 1

Decrement (--)   - Decrease the value by 1

They can also be used as a prefix or preincrement operator where "++" is placed before the variable. This means that 1 is added to the variable's value before it is being used in any other part of the program (the value will be adjusted immediately when used). When "++" is placed after the variable then it becomes a postfix or postincrement operator. This time, 1 is added to the variable's value after the variable is used in any other part of the program (the value will be returned first before it is adjusted).

Example:

MyVariableName = 23;

MyVariableName++;   - returned value is still 23

++MyVariableName;   - returned value is adjusted to 24

Logical Operators

These operators, also called comparison operators, permit a degree of flow control to your program by comparing two values or set specific conditions. A Boolean value can be returned, depending on the two values compared, that will determine whether a certain block of code will be executed or not. This is the most basic form of logic in a computer program.

Is Equal to (==)   - Checks if two values are equal

Is Not Equal to (!=)   - Checks if two values are not equal

Is Greater than (>)   - Checks if the value to the left of the operator is greater than the value to its right

Is Less than (<) - Checks if the value to the left of the operator is less than the

value to its right

Is Greater than or Equal (>=) - Checks if the value to the left of the operator is greater than

or equal to the value to its right

Is Less than or Equal (<=) - Checks if the value to the left of the operator is less than or

equal to the value to its right

Logical AND (&&) - Checks if both values are true

Logical OR (||) - Checks if at least one of the values is true

Bit Wise Operators

These operators manipulate variables at the bit level in a primitive yet fast way. Since they analyze binary numerals, which are the smallest unit of addressable memory, they process execution in the quickest way possible.

And (&)   - A 2 equal-length binary operator
that performs with the logic operator

> "AND" and multiplies both
> elements with bits

Not (~)   - A unary operator that performs
with the goal of logical negation and

> complements the binary
> value of ones

Or (|)   - An operator that takes 2-bit
patterns whose lengths are equal and

> performs with the logic
> operator "OR" (results are either 0
> or 1)

Xor (^)   - An operator that takes 2-bit
patterns whose lengths are equal (results are

> expected to be defined with
> a similar digit)

Now that you have learned how to manipulate operators, you will be more adept in understanding and automating more complex Java programs. Another programming feature that will be introduced in the next chapter is flow control, which demonstrates non-sequential lines of codes.

Chapter Seven: Flow Control

This chapter will emphasize on a non-sequential method of Java programming. You will get acquainted with the if-then-else and different loop statements.

With our previous simple program examples, we were oriented that a Java class is executed in one direction – from the topmost line of code up to the bottom, or what we call sequential programming. However, there will be cases that you will be required to write codes in a non-sequential fashion, especially for those more complicated scenarios. This is accomplished using logical and looping statements, so you can control the flow of your program to perform more complex functions.

If-Then-Else

This is the most basic flow control statement that uses logical operators to determine whether or not a specific condition is fulfilled. Let us add an if-then-else statement to our first simple java program that will display whether the user is a minor or not based on the age that he has provided. By the way, in this example, one is considered a minor if the age is below 18 years old.

```
                                    Java - Example/src/Example.java - Eclipse
File  Edit  Source  Refactor  Navigate  Search  Project  Run  Window  Help

    Example.java

import java.util.Scanner;
public class Example {
// A Java program begins with a call to main().
    public static void main(String args[]){

        int MyVariableName = 0;
        System.out.println("Java is essential to the Web");
        System.out.println("How old are you?");
        Scanner InputVariableName = new Scanner(System.in);
        MyVariableName = InputVariableName.nextInt();

        if (MyVariableName < 18){
            System.out.println("Your age is " + MyVariableName + " and since it is below 18 then you are considered a minor.");
        }
        else {
            System.out.println("Your age is " + MyVariableName + " and since it is not below 18 then you are not a minor anymore.");
        }
    }
}

Console
<terminated> Example [Java Application] C:\Program Files\Java\jre1.8.0_65\bin\javaw.exe (Jan 26, 2016, 2:27:44 PM)
Java is essential to the Web
How old are you?
17
Your age is 17 and since it is below 18 then you are considered a minor.
```

In this new set of programming codes, the condition tested is **if** the value of the user input **MyVariableName** provided is less than 18 or not. If it is, then the methods in the **if block** will be executed - displaying a message on the computer screen that the user is a minor (check the figure above). A block is also called a compound statement. Otherwise, the **else block** will be executed – notifying that the user is not a minor anymore (check the figure below). The **else block** is actually optional, meaning without its codes the program will just proceed to the rest of the class in case the condition is not met. Please take note that the parentheses around the condition and the braces surrounding the statements that are inside the **if** and **else blocks**, are all required. Also notice the indentation of the statements these symbols enclose.

```
import java.util.Scanner;
public class Example {
    // A Java program begins with a call to main().
    public static void main(String args[]){

        int MyVariableName = 0;
        System.out.println("Java is essential to the Web");
        System.out.println("How old are you?");
        Scanner InputVariableName = new Scanner(System.in);
        MyVariableName = InputVariableName.nextInt();

        if (MyVariableName < 18){
            System.out.println("Your age is " + MyVariableName + " and since it is below 18 then you are considered a minor.");
        }
        else {
            System.out.println("Your age is " + MyVariableName + " and since it is not below 18 then you are not a minor anymore.");
        }
    }
}
```

```
Console
<terminated> Example [Java Application] C:\Program Files\Java\jre1.8.0_65\bin\javaw.exe (Jan 26, 2016, 2:28:20 PM)
Java is essential to the Web
How old are you?
Your age is 19 and since it is not below 18 then you are not a minor anymore.
```

Loops

This flow control statement allows methods to be executed over and over again as long as the specific conditions are met. In Java programming language, there are three kinds of loops that can perform repetitive tasks. We will also modify the simple program to do a countdown from 10 to 1 just to demonstrate the syntax for these loops. Again, do not forget the parentheses around the conditions, the braces and the indentations.

While loop – Considered as the simplest kind of "event driven" loop, this statement will execute the methods inside the **while block** as long as the specific conditions are met. Depending on the conditions set, this loop may never run even once.

File   Edit   Source   Refactor   Navigate   Search   Project   Run   Window   Help

```
X .project      J *Example.java

   /*
    * This is a simple Java program.
    *
    * Call this file Example.java
    */
   import java.util.Scanner;
   public class Example {
   // A Java program begins with a call to main().
       public static void main(String args[]){

           int MyVariableName = 10;
           System.out.println("Java is essential to the Web");
           while (MyVariableName > 0){
               System.out.println(MyVariableName);
               MyVariableName--;
           }
       }
   }
```

Console

<terminated> Example [Java Application] C:\Program Files\Java\jre1.8.0_65\bin\javaw.exe (Jan 26, 2016, 9:34:58 PM)

```
Java is essential to the Web
10
9
8
7
6
5
4
3
2
1
```

In the program example above, the **MyVariableName** was first set to a value of 10. Next, the loop will check that while the variable is greater than 0, the program will display the value of the **MyVariableName** in every new line and then decrement it by 1. This will continue to run until **MyVariableName** is equal to 0. If at the start of program execution, the value of **MyVariableName** is already equal or less than 0, then the while loop will be bypassed.

Do-while loop – The main difference between this and a while loop is that the methods inside the do-while loop is sure to run at least once before the condition is checked. In contrast with the while loop, the do loop's condition is indicated at the bottom (this is the primary reason why the loop statement is executed at least one time)

```java
/*
 * This is a simple Java program.
 *
 * Call this file Example.java
 */
import java.util.Scanner;
public class Example {
    // A Java program begins with a call to main().
    public static void main(String args[]) {
        int MyVariableName = 10;
        System.out.println("Java is essential to the Web");
        do {
            System.out.println(MyVariableName);
            MyVariableName--;
        }
        while (MyVariableName > 0);
    }
}
```

Console
<terminated> Example [Java Application] C:\Program Files\Java\jre1.8.0_65\bin\javaw.exe (Jan 26, 2016, 9:39:19 PM)
```
Java is essential to the Web
10
9
8
7
6
5
4
3
2
1
```

In the program example above, again, the variable **MyVariableName** was first set to a value of 10. In the succeeding loop statement, no condition is checked yet. Instead, the **do block** will have to display the value of **MyVariableName**

78

in every new line and then decrement it by 1 before the while condition is checked. This is what was discussed earlier that loop will definitely run once whether or not the conditions are met. Please take note of the semicolon at the right of the condition.

For loop – This statement is declared with specific parameters that control as to when or how many times the methods are to be executed. Variables that can be used to control the loop may be declared simultaneously within the loop itself. The form of the for loop statement is:

for (initialization; condition; iteration) statement;

The initialization part sets a loop control variable to an initial value. The condition is a Boolean expression that tests the loop control variable whether it is true or false. If the result of that test is true, then the execution of the for loop is continuously repeated. If it is false, then the loop stops.

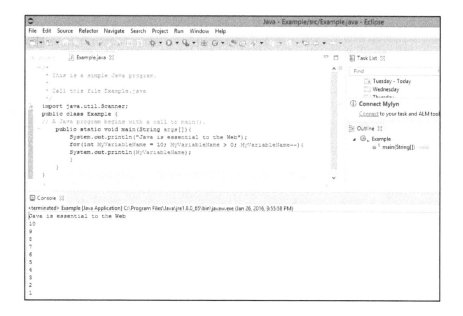

In this final example, you will notice that all the parameters were set at the beginning, when the **for loop** statement was declared. So in the **for loop** declaration, **MyVariableName** was set to a value of 10, the condition whether it is greater than 0 is checked and then decrement its value by 1. After all these lines of code are performed or executed then the value of **MyVariableName** is displayed into the screen, each value on a separate line

In reality, there are usually a multitude of ways to accomplish a certain programming task. However, a good practice as a programmer is always to code your programs in an elegant way that entails choosing the most appropriate loop. One has the option to be creative and flexible, but this sometimes this leads to confusion.

Through this chapter, you have realized that Java programming is not only one-directional by integrating flow control through various looping statements. In the succeeding chapter, you will have a clearer image of what access modifiers are.

Chapter Eight: Access Modifiers

We have already been talking about Java variables, classes, fields and methods. Whenever they are declared you will have to indicate how they are controlled and how they are accessed in the entire program. Whether they are restricted or not, their accessibility feature will be determined by access modifiers that this chapter will take a closer look at.

Deciding on what modifier to use depends on your program's goal and what you are really trying to achieve. The following are the different types of modifiers:

Default

This is the type that is assigned when there is no access modifier specified. Due to its absence, any command or function can access a part of the program. However, its availability is only limited to access by fields that belong to a similar package. A program without a modifier can look effective but not quite clean. The level of access is usually open to the public but it is not included in an interface.

Example:

String version = " 1.00.1"

Boolean process_order () {

       Return true

}

In this example, the program declared a string order version at the beginning. Since a specific type of access modifier is undefined, any command of function can be used to access the program component. Therefore, **process_order** can be modified easily.

Private

This is the type of modifier that accommodates the most restrictive fields in the program. It cannot be accessed, thus, cannot also be used by any command or function. Let's say a particular instruction is from an unlisted source, it cannot be granted recognition.

Example:

```
public class arcadia extends bay {

        private int name_of_residents
        private boolean in_city

        public arcadia () {
                name_of_residents = joy
                in_city = false
        }

        private void shrill ()
        system.out.printIn (quiet);

        public void action ()
        system.out.printIn (talk);
}
```

For this example, the program defined a public class arcadia, which is allowed an extensive function bay. Although arcadia bay is set to public, some of its internal properties are set to private. In addition, since one of its internal components (action) is set to public, it can be acknowledged by different fields.

Public

This is the type of modifier that allows access from about any other field. With a public access level, it is less troublesome for a programmer to visit other parts of his work. All the commands, functions and different components of the program belonging to the public class can be accessed through a recognized set of instructions in Java programming language. However, being publicly declared has some drawbacks or limitations. Even if all the commands and functions are set to public, they cannot be accessed by classes that belong to a different package.

Example:

```
public static void (string arguments) {

}
```

Protected

This type of access modifier belongs to what we call a superclass and is characterized by being less hidden and secure as compared to the default type. It also signifies two things:

- it can only be accessed by the fields that are declared in a particular superclass
- it can only be accessed by the subclasses of a similar package

Such categorization is implemented to improve program structure while limiting the access of an irrelevant element. Protected access modifiers also impose strict protocols and the application is limited (cannot be applied to classes and interfaces). If a field is not connected to any class or interface, then it can declared as protected.

Example:

class seven_fields

protected boolean open_fields (field1 sp) {

// implementation

}

Class opening seven_fields (field1 sp) {

// implementation

}

In this example, class seven_fields was declared and since it is under the protected access modifier, its Boolean logic open_fields is inaccessible with the use of just any function or command. Unless a new access modifier is declared, this particular part of the program cannot be modified.

You have learnt from this chapter that whatever you want to achieve in developing a Java program will determine the appropriate type of access modifier to be used. Each of the four types of access modifiers has its own characteristic and functionality that will affect how objects are accessed in a given Java program. We will now take a closer look at the possible class variables and objects in the next chapter.

Chapter Nine: Classes and Objects

You have already been encountering Java classes and objects in the previous chapters of this eBook. At this point in time, you will gain more knowledge on the available class variables and objects that you can employ to achieve the desired results of why you are programming in a Java environment.

Classes

Acting as blueprints of a Java program, classes are templates that describe the characteristics of an element or method. Basically, they are generic elements in Java programming. They also help a programmer to understand the coding system of another programmer, making its structure clear. Classes exist in the program as long as they desire, meaning they do not have a lifespan.

The following is a list of possible class variables:

- Class - A class is a variable that needs to be declared before it enters a class, which can be found within any class and outside any method.

- Instance - Instance is a variable that remains within a particular class but is outside a method. However, it is accessible from any other method once declared.

- Local - A local is a variable that is defined inside any method in the program and requires initial declaration and acknowledgement. It is omitted after it has executed the command or function.

Objects

Java objects are elements that possess behaviors and states. When elements are defined, they come with their own features that further adds value to a program component without having to include an extensive feature. These are what you call instances of classes. Because of the behaviors and states of objects, methods are executed successfully. Furthermore, a particular object is associated with a unique function or command so it will adhere to certain instructions. In contrast with a class, an object ceases to exist once the program has been executed.

One of the characteristics of object-oriented programming is organizing things and concepts. There are three object relationships that defines why elements should or should not be moved to another particular program component:

- Is-a Relationship – this means that a type of object is more specific than its fellows (number 1 *is a* number)

- Has-a relationship – this means that a type of object contains or is associated with another object (given number 1 and number 2: number 1 *has a* succeeding number, number 2)

- Uses-a relationship – this means that a type of object will be using another object as a program progresses (given number 1, number 2 and number 3: number 1 *uses a* number 2 to arrive at the sum of number 3)

It is important that you know how to work around with classes and objects when programming using the Java language since they are considered as the generic elements of the software. You have also learned how they are organized and their existing relationships with one another. For the last but not the least chapter, you will be given an idea on what constructors are all about.

Chapter Ten: Constructors

One of the many Java concepts that this chapter introduces is the importance of constructors. Constructors are one of the many method-like things that allow the declaration of elements or the creation of new objects.

Constructors work as commands that need to match the other elements in a predefined function whenever they are invoked. They are also either defined or provided by default in Java programming language. Default constructors can set parameters but are not designed to carry out specific tasks nor perform unique actions. They cannot even take any argument. An explicit version of a constructor is required to allow the execution of particular commands and functions.

The main goal of constructors is to initialize the call to a fellow constructor by declaring **special ()**. Upon the acknowledgement of a new constructor, a programmer is encouraged to create and set a parameter for the introduction of an object.

This

This constructor is used to pertain to a particular program component and most of the time it is used as reference to other constructors in a similar class, but in different parameter list.

Example:

```
public class dolphin {
        string name;
        dolphin (string input) {

dolphin () {
        this ("kevin / kim");
}

public static void int main (string arguments []) {
        dolphin p1 = new dolphin ("abigail")
        dolphin p2 = new dolphin ();
        }
}
```

In the example above, the constructor use of **this** refers to other constructors named **kevin** and **kim** under the public class dolphin. The strings have declared arguments and two batches of parameters are set – **abigail** for **p1** and default constructor for **p2**.

Super

This constructor is usually identified in the first line of the programming code since Java compilers do not return a value if **super** is not declared initially. This keyword invokes a superclass constructor.

Example:

```
public class super superclass_penta {
        super superclass_penta [] {}
}
class tonics extends superclass_penta
        tonics () {
                super [];
        }
```

In this example, **super** was used as a constructor that defines superclass_penta. It is categorized under the class **tonics**. Although a class is already known to be previously defined, the capability of a special constructor performance is possible.

This chapter has explained to you two constructors that you can use in Java programming – **this** and **super**. It is imperative that you know when to use these constructors for your program to run properly.

Here is a quick recap of what we covered in case you need a refresher on a certain step:

1. You now have an understanding of how Java technology was developed

2. You learnt how to install and setup Java software and other required program tools

3. You learnt how to create a simple Java program

4. You learnt how to include a user input feature in your Java program

5. You learnt how to properly declare and manipulate variables

6. You learnt how to modify the complexity of your Java program through operators

7. You learnt how to perform non-sequential programming using flow control statements

8. You learnt how to differentiate and use appropriately Java access modifiers

9. You learnt how to work around with classes and objects

10. You also learnt how to correctly employ constructors in your Java program

Practice Exercises

Exercise #1:

Write a program that will display every command-line argument and the total number of arguments.

CLUE: Use an array variable named *length* to determine the length of the array.

Exercise #2:

Write a program that will round off a series of ten random numbers from 0 to 100. Round each one of them, then display the result to the screen. Take note of the following:

- Create a *class* and a *main()* method for the calculation.
- Use the *for loop* statement.
- Use the *Math.random()* to generate the ten random numbers. To get a number between 0 to 100, simply multiply the random number by 100.
- Round the number using the *Math.round()* method. Rounding off is necessary because the *random()* method always returns a value less than 1.0.
- Display the rounded number to the screen.

Exercise #3:

Write a program that will create a new *Parent* class under a main *Family* class. The objective is also to display the line of text "What a wonderful day!" on the screen.

Practice Exercises Answers

Answer for Exercise #1:

```
public class MainPractice {
        public static void main (String [] args) {
                for (int i = 0; i < args.length; i++) {
                        System.out.println(args[i]);
                }
                System.out.print("Total Words: " +
args.length);
        }
}
```

Answer for Exercise #2:

```
public class MathRandomRound {
        public static void main (String [] argh) {
                for (int i = 0; i < 10; i++) {
                        double num = Math.random() *
100;
                        System.out.print("The number " +
num);
                        System.out.println(" rounds to " +
Math.round(num));
                }
        }
}
```

Answer for Exercise #3:

```
class Parent {

}

public class Family {
        public static void main(String[] args) {
                System.out.println("What a wonderful day!");
                Parent parent = new Parent();
        }
}
```

Before You Go!

I hope that you have enjoyed learning the basics of Java programming through this eBook and have tremendously benefited from reading it. I have ensured that my goal was met in writing this – to offer great value for your money without cutting corners in educating you what Java is all about. I believe you will now be confident enough in creating your very own Java program by following the guidelines I have included in this eBook.

I would also strongly recommend that you learn other programming languages so that you may be able to take your knowledge to the next and become a top-class programmer and because you have gone through this course, you will be astonished to find that your learning other languages is easier than expected, for JavaScript has strikingly paved the way for you. You can find other popular programming books by visiting our full library at >> http://amzn.to/1Xxmab2

I would now really appreciate your reviews and your feedback. If you really enjoyed this book, then feel free to share it so other people may also profit from this information.

To leave a review, please visit http://amzn.to/1Rob2uH

Before You Go, Here Are Other Books Our Readers Loved!

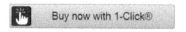

http://amzn.to/1WI6fHu

Learn R Programming
With This Easy,
Step-By-Step Guide

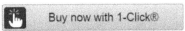

http://amzn.to/24XxoLM

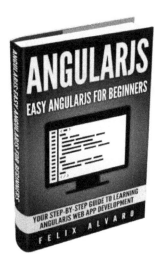

Learn AngularJS
Web-App Developing
Today With This Easy,
Step-By-Step Guide

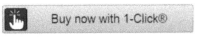

http://amzn.to/1pDq0BZ

Learn Python Programming Today With This Easy, Step-By-Step Guide!

http://amzn.to/1WOBiy2

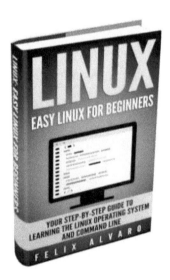

Learn The Linux Operating System and Command Line Today!

http://amzn.to/1QzQPkY

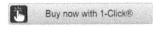
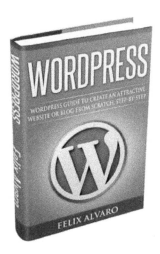

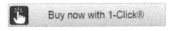

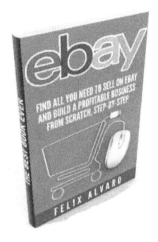

Launch Your Own Profitable eBay Business- Learn Everything You Need to Know to Get Started Today!

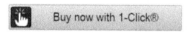

http://amzn.to/1R1vnCP

Finally, you can also send me an email if you have any questions, feedback or just want to say hello! (I do reply!) My email address is; (Felix_Alvaro@mail.com)

I thank you once again and God bless!

Felix Alvaro

www.ingramcontent.com/pod-product-compliance
Lightning Source LLC
LaVergne TN
LVHW052306060326
832902LV00021B/3727